This book belongs to an awesome dancer called:

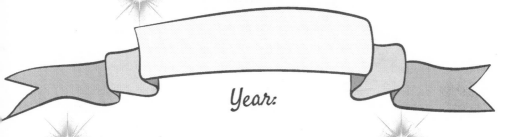

Year:

Remember, everything you need to
be great is already inside you

About Me

Age ___ Grade ___ Studio/School: _____

Favorite dance style: _____

Best dance move: _____

Favorite song: _____

Favorite dancer: _____

Dance Coach / Teacher: _____

Strengths:

Persistence ☐ Expression ☐ Technicality ☐ Balance ☐

Flexibility ☐ Musicality ☐ Other ☐ _____

Goals for the Year

_____
_____
_____
_____

I promise to improve on

_____
_____

Notes _____

_____
_____

I love my dance Studio / School because

_____

_____

Favorite famous dancer _____

Favorite Instructor _____

My Dance Friends _____

_____

Funniest _____

Chattiest _____

Bravest _____

My favorite Costume

Color

_____

Design

_____

Accessories

_____

Class Schedule

Class Schedule

December

Week 1

Priorities

Monday

Tuesday

Wednesday

Thursday

Friday

Saturday

To Do

★

★

★

★

★

Notes

My Dance Week

Instructor Name: _____

Hours put in : _____

Achievements: _____

How I felt   ☹ 😕 😐 🙂 😄

Conditioning notes:

Move:	Rep:

Instructor Said:

Best thing this week:

I am grateful for

January

Week 2

Sometimes later becomes never. Do it now.

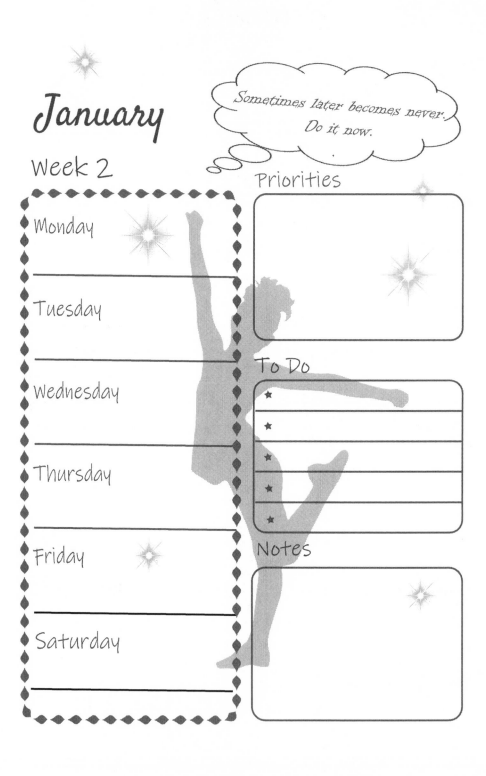

Monday

Tuesday

Wednesday

Thursday

Friday

Saturday

Priorities

To Do

★
★
★
★
★

Notes

My Dance Week

Instructor Name: _____

Hours put in : _____

Achievements: _____

How I felt ☹ 🙂 😐 🙂 😃

Conditioning notes:

Move:	Rep:

Instructor Said:

Best thing this Week:

I am grateful for

January

Week 3

Great things never come from comfort zones.

Monday

Tuesday

Wednesday

Thursday

Friday

Saturday

Priorities

To Do

★
★
★
★
★

Notes

My Dance Week

Instructor Name: _____

Hours put in : _____

Achievements: _____

How I felt   ☹ 😕 😐 🙂 😃

Conditioning notes:

Move:	Rep:

Instructor Said:

Best thing this week:

I am grateful for

January

Week 4

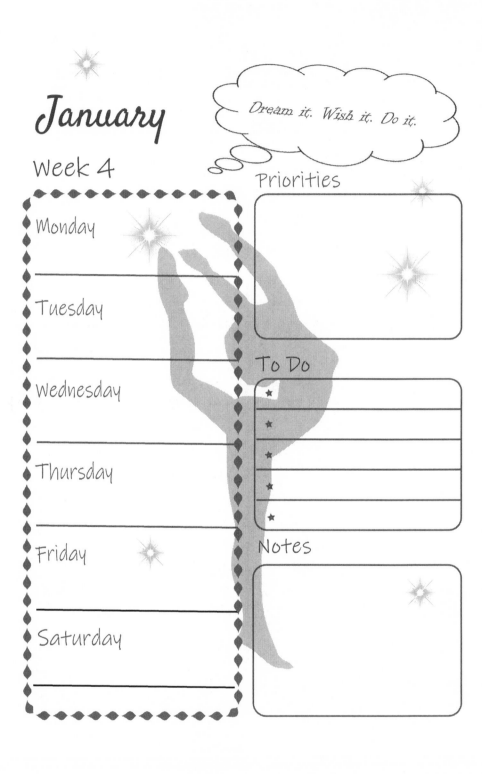

Dream it. Wish it. Do it.

Monday

Tuesday

Wednesday

Thursday

Friday

Saturday

Priorities

To Do

Notes

My Dance Week

Instructor Name: _____

Hours put in : _____

Achievements: _____

How I felt   ☹ 🙁 😐 🙂 😄

Conditioning notes:

Move:	Rep:

Instructor Said:

Best thing this week:

I am
grateful for

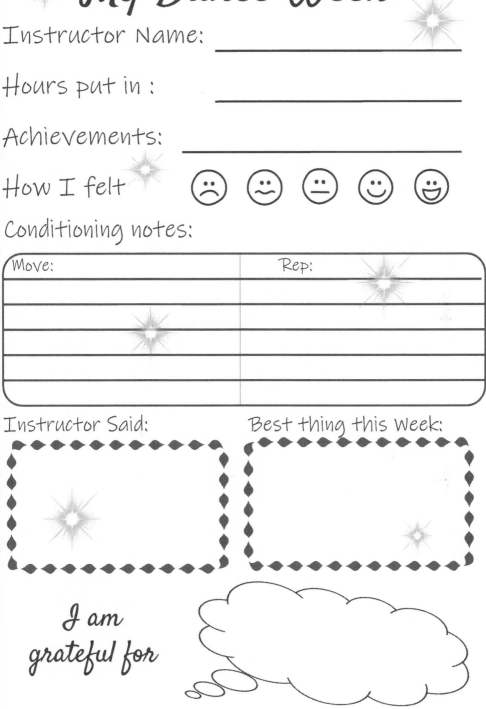

January

Week 5

Monday

Tuesday

Wednesday

Thursday

Friday

Saturday

Priorities

To Do

- ★
- ★
- ★
- ★
- ★

Notes

My Dance Week

Instructor Name: _____

Hours put in : _____

Achievements: _____

How I felt   ☹ 😕 😐 🙂 😃

Conditioning notes:

Move:	Rep:

Instructor Said:

Best thing this Week:

I am grateful for

February

Week 6

Monday

Tuesday

Wednesday

Thursday

Friday

Saturday

Priorities

To Do

- ★
- ★
- ★
- ★
- ★

Notes

My Dance Week

Instructor Name: _____

Hours put in : _____

Achievements: _____

How I felt 😦 🙁 😐 🙂 😃

Conditioning notes:

Move:	Rep:

Instructor Said:

Best thing this week:

I am
grateful for

February

Week 7

Monday

Tuesday

Wednesday

Thursday

Friday

Saturday

Priorities

To Do

★

★

★

★

★

Notes

My Dance Week

Instructor Name: _____

Hours put in : _____

Achievements: _____

How I felt ☹ 😕 😐 🙂 😀

Conditioning notes:

Move:	Rep:

Instructor Said:

Best thing this week:

I am grateful for

February

Week 8

Wake up with determination.
Go to bed with satisfaction.

Monday

Tuesday

Wednesday

Thursday

Friday

Saturday

Priorities

To Do

- ★
- ★
- ★
- ★
- ★

Notes

My Dance Week

Instructor Name: _____

Hours put in : _____

Achievements: _____

How I felt   ☹️ 🙁 😐 🙂 😃

Conditioning notes:

Move:	Rep:

Instructor Said:

Best thing this week:

I am
grateful for

February

Week 9

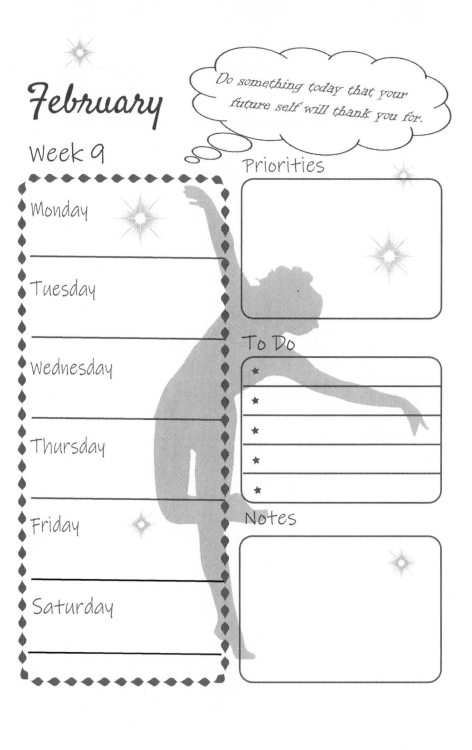

Monday

Tuesday

Wednesday

Thursday

Friday

Saturday

Priorities

To Do

- ★
- ★
- ★
- ★
- ★

Notes

My Dance Week

Instructor Name: _____

Hours put in : _____

Achievements: _____

How I felt   ☹ 😕 😐 🙂 😀

Conditioning notes:

Move:	Rep:

Instructor Said:

Best thing this week:

I am grateful for

March

Week 10

Little things make big days.

Monday

Tuesday

Wednesday

Thursday

Friday

Saturday

Priorities

To Do

- ★
- ★
- ★
- ★
- ★

Notes

My Dance Week

Instructor Name: _____

Hours put in : _____

Achievements: _____

How I felt 😟 🙂 😐 😊 😃

Conditioning notes:

Move:	Rep:

Instructor Said:

Best thing this week:

I am grateful for

March

Week 11

It's going to be hard, but hard does not mean impossible.

Monday

Tuesday

Wednesday

Thursday

Friday

Saturday

Priorities

To Do
- ★
- ★
- ★
- ★
- ★

Notes

My Dance Week

Instructor Name: _____

Hours put in : _____

Achievements: _____

How I felt ☹ 😕 😐 🙂 😃

Conditioning notes:

Move:	Rep:

Instructor Said:

Best thing this week:

I am grateful for

March

Week 12

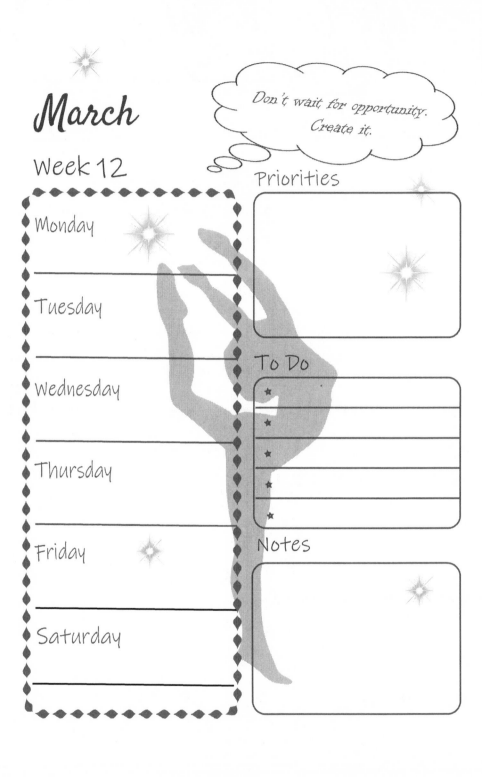

Don't wait for opportunity. Create it.

Monday

Tuesday

Wednesday

Thursday

Friday

Saturday

Priorities

To Do

- ★
- ★
- ★
- ★
- ★

Notes

My Dave Week

Instructor Name: _____

Hours put in : _____

Achievements: _____

How I felt ☹️ 😕 😐 🙂 😄

Conditioning notes:

Move:	Rep:

Instructor Said:

Best thing this week:

I am grateful for

March

Week 13

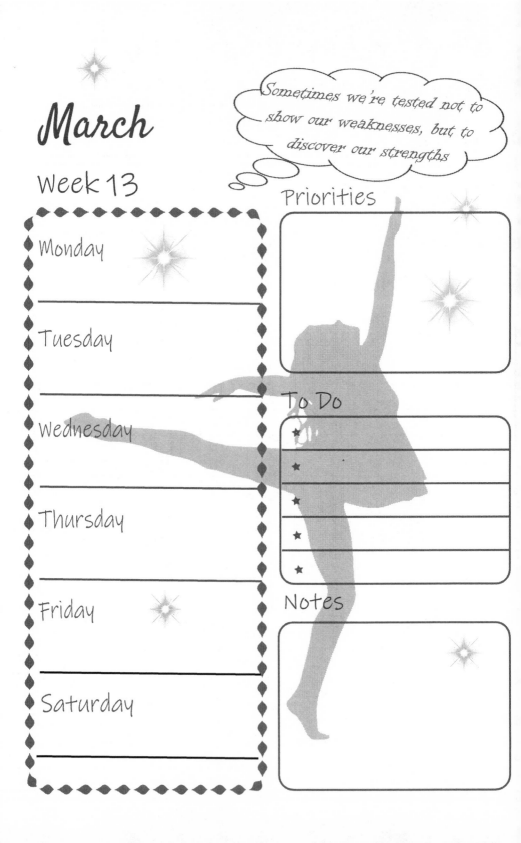

Sometimes we're tested not to show our weaknesses, but to discover our strengths

Monday

Tuesday

Wednesday

Thursday

Friday

Saturday

Priorities

To Do

★
★
★
★
★

Notes

My Dance Week

Instructor Name: _____

Hours put in : _____

Achievements: _____

How I felt ☹ 🙁 😐 🙂 😃

Conditioning notes:

Move:	Rep:

Instructor Said:

Best thing this week:

I am grateful for

April

Week 14

The key to success is to focus on goals, not obstacles.

Monday

Tuesday

Wednesday

Thursday

Friday

Saturday

Priorities

To Do

★
★
★
★
★

Notes

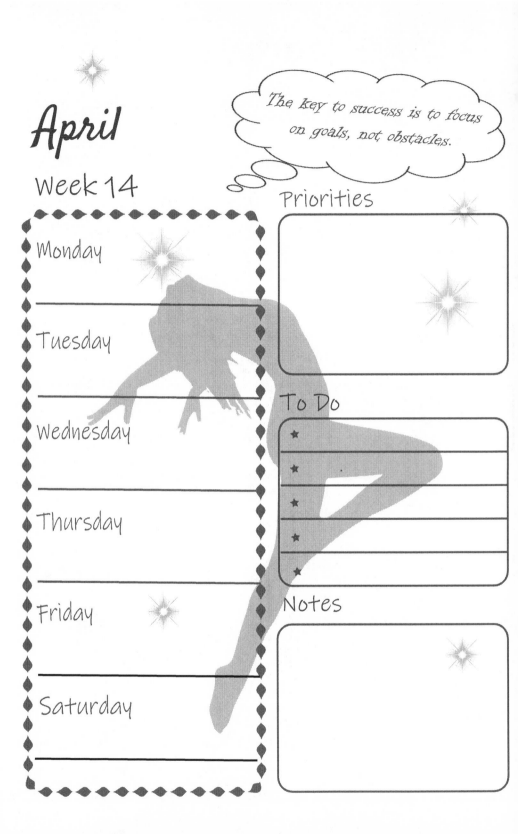

My Dance Week

Instructor Name: _____

Hours put in : _____

Achievements: _____

How I felt ☹ 🙂 😐 🙂 😃

Conditioning notes:

Move:	Rep:

Instructor Said:

Best thing this week:

I am
grateful for

April

Week 15

Monday

Tuesday

Wednesday

Thursday

Friday

Saturday

Priorities

To Do

★

★

★

★

★

Notes

My Dance Week

Instructor Name: _____

Hours put in : _____

Achievements: _____

How I felt ☹ 🙁 😐 🙂 😃

Conditioning notes:

Move:	Rep:

Instructor Said:

Best thing this week:

I am grateful for

April

Week 16

Monday

Tuesday

Wednesday

Thursday

Friday

Saturday

Priorities

TO DO

★
★
★
★
★

Notes

My Dance Week

Instructor Name: _____

Hours put in : _____

Achievements: _____

How I felt ☹ ☺ 😐 ☺ 😃

Conditioning notes:

Move:	Rep:

Instructor Said:

Best thing this Week:

I am grateful for

April

Week 17

Monday

Tuesday

Wednesday

Thursday

Friday

Saturday

Priorities

To Do

- ★
- ★
- ★
- ★
- ★

Notes

My Dance Week

Instructor Name: _____

Hours put in : _____

Achievements: _____

How I felt ☹ 😕 😐 🙂 😀

Conditioning notes:

Move:	Rep:

Instructor Said:

Best thing this week:

I am grateful for

April

Week 18

Monday

Tuesday

Wednesday

Thursday

Friday

Saturday

Priorities

To Do

- ★
- ★
- ★
- ★
- ★

Notes

My Dance Week

Instructor Name: _____

Hours put in : _____

Achievements: _____

How I felt 😞 😟 😐 🙂 😄

Conditioning notes:

Move:	Rep:

Instructor Said:

Best thing this week:

I am grateful for

May

Week 19

Play like you are in first.
Train like you are in second.

Monday

Tuesday

Wednesday

Thursday

Friday

Saturday

Priorities

To Do

★
★
★
★
★

Notes

My Dance Week

Instructor Name: _____

Hours put in : _____

Achievements: _____

How I felt ☹ 🙂 😐 🙂 😀

Conditioning notes:

Move:	Rep:

Instructor Said:

Best thing this week:

I am
grateful for

May

Week 20

I can and I will.

Priorities

Monday

Tuesday

Wednesday

To Do

★

★

★

★

★

Thursday

Friday

Notes

Saturday

My Dance Week

Instructor Name: _____

Hours put in : _____

Achievements: _____

How I felt   ☹ 🙂 😐 🙂 😄

Conditioning notes:

Move:	Rep:

Instructor Said:

Best thing this Week:

I am grateful for

May

Week 21

Monday

Tuesday

Wednesday

Thursday

Friday

Saturday

It never gets easier - you just get better.

Priorities

To Do

- ★
- ★
- ★
- ★
- ★

Notes

My Dance Week

Instructor Name: _____

Hours put in : _____

Achievements: _____

How I felt 😦 🙂 😐 🙂 😃

Conditioning notes:

Move:	Rep:

Instructor Said:

Best thing this week:

I am grateful for

May

Week 22

Monday

Tuesday

Wednesday

Thursday

Friday

Saturday

Priorities

To Do

★
★
★
★
★

Notes

My Dance Week

Instructor Name: _____

Hours put in : _____

Achievements: _____

How I felt ☹ 🙂 😐 🙂 😃

Conditioning notes:

Move:	Rep:

Instructor Said:

Best thing this week:

I am grateful for

June

Week 23

Monday

Tuesday

Wednesday

Thursday

Friday

Saturday

Priorities

To Do

- ★
- ★
- ★
- ★
- ★

Notes

My Dance Week

Instructor Name: _____

Hours put in : _____

Achievements: _____

How I felt   ☹ 😕 😐 🙂 😄

Conditioning notes:

Move:	Rep:

Instructor Said:

Best thing this week:

I am grateful for

June

Week 24

If you don't leap, you'll never know what it's like to fly

Monday

Tuesday

Wednesday

Thursday

Friday

Saturday

Priorities

To Do

★

★

Notes

My Dance Week

Instructor Name: _____

Hours put in: _____

Achievements: _____

How I felt 😦 🙂 😐 🙂 😄

Conditioning notes:

Move:	Rep:

Instructor Said:

Best thing this week:

I am grateful for

June

Week 25

Monday

Tuesday

Wednesday

Thursday

Friday

Saturday

Priorities

To Do

★

★

★

★

★

Notes

My Dance Week

Instructor Name: _____

Hours put in : _____

Achievements: _____

How I felt   ☹ 🙂 😐 🙂 😃

Conditioning notes:

Move:	Rep:

Instructor Said:

Best thing this week:

I am grateful for

June

Week 26

Monday

Tuesday

Wednesday

Thursday

Friday

Saturday

Priorities

To Do

★
★
★
★
★

Notes

My Dance Week

Instructor Name: _____

Hours put in : _____

Achievements: _____

How I felt ☹ 🙁 😐 🙂 😀

Conditioning notes:

Move:	Rep:

Instructor Said:

Best thing this Week:

I am grateful for

July

Week 27

Monday

Tuesday

Wednesday

Thursday

Friday

Saturday

Priorities

To Do

- ★
- ★
- ★
- ★
- ★

Notes

My Dance Week

Instructor Name: _____

Hours put in : _____

Achievements: _____

How I felt ☹ 😕 😐 🙂 😀

Conditioning notes:

Move:	Rep:

Instructor Said:

Best thing this week:

I am grateful for

July

Week 28

Monday

Tuesday

Wednesday

Thursday

Friday

Saturday

Priorities

To Do

- ★
- ★
- ★
- ★
- ★

Notes

My Dance Week

Instructor Name: _____

Hours put in : _____

Achievements: _____

How I felt ☹ 🙁 😐 🙂 😃

Conditioning notes:

Move:	Rep:

Instructor Said:

Best thing this Week:

I am grateful for

July

Week 29

Monday

Tuesday

Wednesday

Thursday

Friday

Saturday

Priorities

To Do

- ★
- ★
- ★
- ★
- ★

Notes

My Dance Week

Instructor Name: _____

Hours put in : _____

Achievements: _____

How I felt

Conditioning notes:

Move:	Rep:

Instructor Said:

Best thing this week:

I am grateful for

July

Week 30

Forget the mistake - remember the lesson.

Monday

Tuesday

Wednesday

Thursday

Friday

Saturday

Priorities

To Do

★
★
★
★ .
★

Notes

Forget the mistake – remember the lesson.

My Dance Week

Instructor Name: _____

Hours put in : _____

Achievements: _____

How I felt ☹ 🙂 😐 🙂 😄

Conditioning notes:

Move:	Rep:

Instructor Said:

Best thing this Week:

I am grateful for

July

Week 31

Monday

Tuesday

Wednesday

Thursday

Friday

Saturday

Work hard - dream big.

Priorities

To Do

★

★

★

★

★

Notes

My Dance Week

Instructor Name: _____

Hours put in : _____

Achievements: _____

How I felt   ☹ 😐 😐 🙂 😀

Conditioning notes:

Move:	Rep:

Instructor Said: Best thing this week:

I am grateful for

August

Week 32

Make it happen –
shock everyone.

Priorities

Monday

Tuesday

Wednesday

Thursday

Friday

Saturday

To Do

★

★

★

Notes

My Dance Week

Instructor Name: _____

Hours put in : _____

Achievements: _____

How I felt ☹ 😕 😐 🙂 😃

Conditioning notes:

Move:	Rep:

Instructor Said:

Best thing this week:

I am grateful for

August

Week 33

Look in the mirror – that's your competition.

Monday

Tuesday

Wednesday

Thursday

Friday

Saturday

Priorities

To Do

- ★
- ★
- ★
- ★
- ★

Notes

My Dance Week

Instructor Name: _____

Hours put in : _____

Achievements: _____

How I felt ☹ 🙂 😐 🙂 😁

Conditioning notes:

Move:	Rep:

Instructor Said:

Best thing this Week:

I am grateful for

August

Week 34

Monday

Tuesday

Wednesday

Thursday

Friday

Saturday

Priorities

To Do

★
★
★
★
★

Notes

My Dance Week

Instructor Name: _____

Hours put in : _____

Achievements: _____

How I felt

Conditioning notes:

Move:	Rep:

Instructor Said:

Best thing this week:

I am
grateful for

August

Week 35

Monday

Tuesday

Wednesday

Thursday

Friday

Saturday

Be driven.

Priorities

To Do

- ★
- ★
- ★
- ★
- ★

Notes

My Dance Week

Instructor Name: _____

Hours put in : _____

Achievements: _____

How I felt   ☹ 🙂 😐 🙂 😃

Conditioning notes:

Move:	Rep:

Instructor Said: Best thing this Week:

I am grateful for

September

Week 36

Be hungry.

Priorities

Monday

Tuesday

Wednesday

Thursday

Friday

Saturday

To Do

- ★
- ★
- ★
- ★
- ★

Notes

My Dance Week

Instructor Name: _____

Hours put in : _____

Achievements: _____

How I felt ☹️ 🙂 😐 🙂 😃

Conditioning notes:

Move:	Rep:

Instructor Said:

Best thing this week:

*I am
grateful for*

September

Week 37

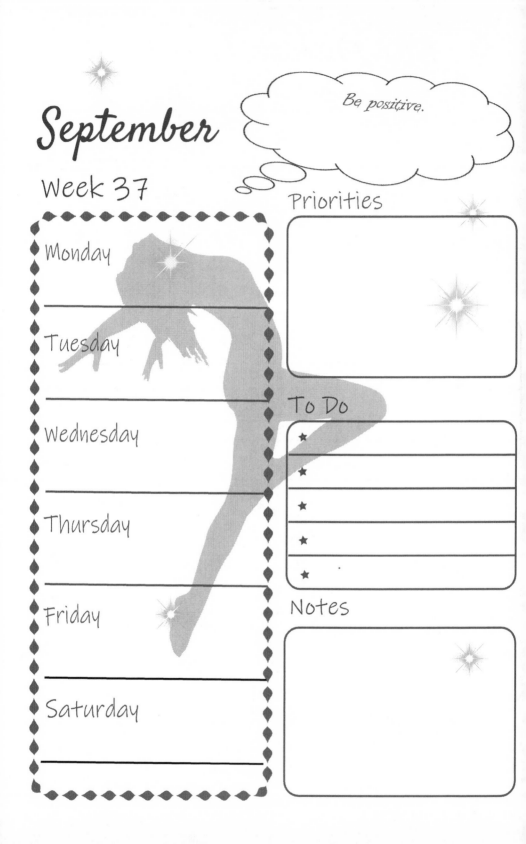

Be positive.

Monday

Tuesday

Wednesday

Thursday

Friday

Saturday

Priorities

To Do

- ★
- ★
- ★
- ★
- ★

Notes

My Dance Week

Instructor Name: _____

Hours put in : _____

Achievements: _____

How I felt   ☹ 😕 😐 🙂 😃

Conditioning notes:

Move:	Rep:

Instructor Said:

Best thing this Week:

I am grateful for

September

Week 38

Monday

Tuesday

Wednesday

Thursday

Friday

Saturday

Priorities

To Do

- ★
- ★
- ★
- ★
- ★

Notes

My Dance Week

Instructor Name: _____

Hours put in : _____

Achievements: _____

How I felt   ☹ 🙁 😐 🙂 😃

Conditioning notes:

Move:	Rep:

Instructor Said:

Best thing this Week:

*I am
grateful for*

September

Week 39

Monday

Tuesday

Wednesday

Thursday

Friday

Saturday

Priorities

To Do

- ★
- ★
- ★
- ★
- ★

Notes

My Dance Week

Instructor Name: _____

Hours put in : _____

Achievements: _____

How I felt   ☹ 🙂 😐 🙂 😃

Conditioning notes:

Move:	Rep:

Instructor Said:

Best thing this Week:

I am grateful for

September

Let your mistakes make you better, not bitter.

Week 40

Monday

Tuesday

Wednesday

Thursday

Friday

Saturday

Priorities

To Do

- ★
- ★
- ★
- ★
- ★

Notes

My Dance Week

Instructor Name: _____

Hours put in: _____

Achievements: _____

How I felt 🙁 🙂 😐 🙂 😃

Conditioning notes:

Move:	Rep:

Instructor Said:

Best thing this week:

I am grateful for

October

Week 41

Monday	
Tuesday	
Wednesday	
Thursday	
Friday	
Saturday	

Priorities

To Do

★
★
★
★
★

Notes

My Dunce Week

Instructor Name: _____

Hours put in : _____

Achievements: _____

How I felt ☹ ☺ 😐 🙂 😃

Conditioning notes:

Move:	Rep:

Instructor Said:

Best thing this Week:

I am grateful for

October

Week 42

Monday

Tuesday

Wednesday

Thursday

Friday

Saturday

Priorities

To Do

★

★

Notes

My Dance Week

Instructor Name: _____

Hours put in : _____

Achievements: _____

How I felt ☹ 🙂 😐 🙂 😃

Conditioning notes:

Move:	Rep:

Instructor Said:

Best thing this week:

I am grateful for

October

Week 43

Monday

Tuesday

Wednesday

Thursday

Friday

Saturday

Priorities

To Do

★

★

★

★

★

Notes

My Dance Week

Instructor Name: _____

Hours put in: _____

Achievements: _____

How I felt ☹ 🙂 😐 🙂 😀

Conditioning notes:

Move:	Rep:

Instructor Said:

Best thing this Week:

I am grateful for

October

Week 44

Monday

Tuesday

Wednesday

Thursday

Friday

Saturday

Priorities

To Do

- ★
- ★
- ★
- ★
- ★

Notes

My Dance Week

Instructor Name: _____

Hours put in : _____

Achievements: _____

How I felt ☹ 🙁 😐 🙂 😀

Conditioning notes:

Move:	Rep:

Instructor Said:

Best thing this week:

I am grateful for

November

Week 45

Monday

Tuesday

Wednesday

Thursday

Friday

Saturday

Priorities

To Do

★

★

★

Notes

My Dance Week

Instructor Name: _____

Hours put in : _____

Achievements: _____

How I felt   ☹ 🙁 😐 🙂 😃

Conditioning notes:

Move:	Rep:

Instructor Said:

Best thing this week:

I am grateful for

November

Week 46

Monday

Tuesday

Wednesday

Thursday

Friday

Saturday

Priorities

To Do

★

★

★

★

★

Notes

My Dance Week

Instructor Name: _____

Hours put in : _____

Achievements: _____

How I felt ☹ 😕 😐 🙂 😄

Conditioning notes:

Move:	Rep:

Instructor Said:

Best thing this week:

I am grateful for

November

Week 47

Priorities

Monday

Tuesday

To Do

Wednesday

★

★

★

Thursday

★

★

Friday

Notes

Saturday

My Dance Week

Instructor Name: _____

Hours put in : _____

Achievements: _____

How I felt ☹ 🙁 😐 🙂 😃

Conditioning notes:

Move:	Rep:

Instructor Said:

Best thing this week:

I am grateful for

November

Week 48

Monday

Tuesday

Wednesday

Thursday

Friday

Saturday

Priorities

To Do

★
★
★
★
★

Notes

My Dance Week

Instructor Name: _____

Hours put in : _____

Achievements: _____

How I felt ☹ 🙂 😐 🙂 😃

Conditioning notes:

Move:	Rep:

Instructor Said:

Best thing this week:

I am grateful for

December

Be a light to the world.

Week 49

Monday

Tuesday

Wednesday

Thursday

Friday

Saturday

Priorities

To Do

★

★

★

★

★

Notes

My Dance Week

Instructor Name: _____

Hours put in : _____

Achievements: _____

How I felt ☹ 😐 😑 🙂 😄

Conditioning notes:

Move:	Rep:

Instructor Said:

Best thing this Week:

I am grateful for

December

Week 50

Monday

Tuesday

Wednesday

Thursday

Friday

Saturday

Priorities

To Do

★

★

★

★

★

Notes

My Dance Week

Instructor Name: _____

Hours put in : _____

Achievements: _____

How I felt   ☹   🙁   😐   🙂   😃

Conditioning notes:

Move:	Rep:

Instructor Said: Best thing this week:

I am grateful for

December

Week 51

Monday

Tuesday

Wednesday

Thursday

Friday

Saturday

Priorities

To Do

- ★
- ★
- ★
- ★
- ★

Notes

My Dance Week

Instructor Name: _____

Hours put in : _____

Achievements: _____

How I felt   :) :D

Conditioning notes:

Move:	Rep:

Instructor Said:

Best thing this week:

I am
grateful for

December

Week 52

Priorities

Monday

Tuesday

Wednesday

Thursday

Friday

Saturday

To Do

★
★
★
★
★

Notes

My Dance Week

Instructor Name: _____

Hours put in : _____

Achievements: _____

How I felt   ☹ 🙂 😐 🙂 😄

Conditioning notes:

Move:	Rep:

Instructor Said: Best thing this week:

I am grateful for

My Competitions

Event _____

Location _____ Date _____

Dance:

_____

Score [   ]   Place [   ]

How I felt 😦 😊 😐 🙂 😃

_____

Score [   ]   Place [   ]

How I felt 😦 😊 😐 🙂 😃

_____

Score [   ]   Place [   ]

How I felt 😦 😊 😐 🙂 😃

_____

Score [   ]   Place [   ]

How I felt 😦 😊 😐 🙂 😃

Notes _____

_____

_____

My Competitions

Event _____

Location _____ Date _____

Dance:

_____   Score [   ]   Place [   ]

How I felt   🙁 🙂 😐 🙂 😄

_____   Score [   ]   Place [   ]

How I felt   🙁 🙂 😐 🙂 😄

_____   Score [   ]   Place [   ]

How I felt   🙁 🙂 😐 🙂 😄

_____   Score [   ]   Place [   ]

How I felt   🙁 🙂 😐 🙂 😄

Notes _____

_____

_____

My Competitions

Event _____

Location _____ Date _____

Dance:

_____ Score [   ]   Place [   ]

How I felt 😦 🙂 😐 🙂 😃

_____ Score [   ]   Place [   ]

How I felt 😦 🙂 😐 🙂 😃

_____ Score [   ]   Place [   ]

How I felt 😦 🙂 😐 🙂 😃

_____ Score [   ]   Place [   ]

How I felt 😦 🙂 😐 🙂 😃

Notes _____

_____

_____

My Competitions

Event _____

Location _____ Date _____

Dance:

_____ Score [ ] Place [ ]

How I felt 😦 🙂 😐 😊 😃

_____ Score [ ] Place [ ]

How I felt 😦 🙂 😐 😊 😃

_____ Score [ ] Place [ ]

How I felt 😦 🙂 😐 😊 😃

_____ Score [ ] Place [ ]

How I felt 😦 🙂 😐 😊 😃

Notes _____
_____
_____

My Competitions

Event _____

Location _____ Date _____

Dance:

_____

Score [   ]   Place [   ]

How I felt 😦 😊 😐 🙂 😃

_____

Score [   ]   Place [   ]

How I felt 😦 😊 😐 🙂 😃

_____

Score [   ]   Place [   ]

How I felt 😦 😊 😐 🙂 😃

_____

Score [   ]   Place [   ]

How I felt 😦 😊 😐 🙂 😃

Notes _____

_____

_____

My Competitions

Event _____

Location _____ Date _____

Dance:

_____

Score [   ]   Place [   ]

How I felt   🙁 🙂 😐 🙂 😃

_____

Score [   ]   Place [   ]

How I felt   🙁 🙂 😐 🙂 😃

_____

Score [   ]   Place [   ]

How I felt   🙁 🙂 😐 🙂 😃

_____

Score [   ]   Place [   ]

How I felt   🙁 🙂 😐 🙂 😃

Notes _____

_____

_____

My Competitions

Event _____

Location _____ Date _____

Dance:

_____ Score [ ] Place [ ]

How I felt 😞 😊 😐 🙂 😃

_____ Score [ ] Place [ ]

How I felt 😞 😊 😐 🙂 😃

_____ Score [ ] Place [ ]

How I felt 😞 😊 😐 🙂 😃

_____ Score [ ] Place [ ]

How I felt 😞 😊 😐 🙂 😃

Notes _____

_____

_____

My Competitions

Event _____

Location _____ Date _____

Dance:

_____ Score [   ] Place [   ]

How I felt (☹) (🙁) (😐) (🙂) (😄)

_____ Score [   ] Place [   ]

How I felt (☹) (🙁) (😐) (🙂) (😄)

_____ Score [   ] Place [   ]

How I felt (☹) (🙁) (😐) (🙂) (😄)

_____ Score [   ] Place [   ]

How I felt (☹) (🙁) (😐) (🙂) (😄)

Notes _____

_____

_____

My Competitions

Event _____

Location _____ Date _____

Dance:

_____ Score [ ] Place [ ]

How I felt 🙁 🙂 😐 🙂 😄

_____ Score [ ] Place [ ]

How I felt 🙁 🙂 😐 🙂 😄

_____ Score [ ] Place [ ]

How I felt 🙁 🙂 😐 🙂 😄

_____ Score [ ] Place [ ]

How I felt 🙁 🙂 😐 🙂 😄

Notes _____

_____

_____

My Competitions

Event _____

Location _____ Date _____

Dance:

_____

score [ ]   Place [ ]

How I felt 😦 😕 😐 🙂 😄

_____

Score [ ]   Place [ ]

How I felt 😦 😕 😐 🙂 😄

_____

Score [ ]   Place [ ]

How I felt 😦 😕 😐 🙂 😄

_____

Score [ ]   Place [ ]

How I felt 😦 😕 😐 🙂 😄

Notes _____

_____

_____

Class Schedule